The Lens
I See Through Now

A Personal Perspective on Parenting

April Love-Julien

Copyright page

Dedication

It's amazing how when I started this project, I was not a parent and struggled with infertility. However, upon completing this book, I became a mother. Since becoming a mom, I have found myself becoming more understanding of the many challenges my mother possibly faced!

I would like to dedicate this book to my wonderful mom who, in-spite of her challenges, raised five amazing adults! To my father Jeremiah Travis. I wish we had more time. May you continue to rest peacefully. I love you both forever. I also want to dedicate this book to my amazing husband, Alex Julien, because I get to parent with you. To my two amazing sons, Armarion Julien, and Alex II, for allowing me to change the narrative! I love you three forever.

Acknowledgements

I would like to first thank my Lord and Savior Jesus Christ who continues to show me that I can do all things through Christ who strengthens me! I would like to thank my loving husband, Alex Julien, for being so supportive of me and for being a great example of an amazing husband and parent! To my siblings: Dray, Dula, Al, and Jas—our bond is unmatched, and I appreciate your support!

I would like to thank my grandmother Lola and mother Lora for being my backbone. I am who I am because of you. To my godchildren and many nieces and nephews, I love you all. Thank you to Olivia Shaw-Reel, an amazing author who saw this book to the finish line. You are appreciated!

May this book serve its purpose in bringing awareness to the need for parental presence and involvement. May parents and children everywhere re-examine their relationships. May families unite; may children feel embraced and supported; may parents feel empowered and appreciated and may we all see positive change in our communities. God bless!

Contents

Introduction

Chapter 1: "Supermom" ...The Perfect Parents

Chapter 2: Maybe it's Not Their Fault

Chapter 3: Transparency

Chapter 4: Cycles

Chapter 5: Your Approach

Chapter 6: Listen

Chapter 7: Society Says

Chapter 8: Lessons Learned

Chapter 9: Transitions

Chapter 10: The Outcome

Introduction

One of my favorite songs is Whitney Houston's "The Greatest Love of All." When this book idea came to mind, the opening lyrics would play over and over in my head. Because I was a bonus mother and had not yet conceived a child, I never felt that there was room for me to discuss parenting. However, after the birth of my first son, I felt motivated to revisit the idea. Now, I'm excited to present this book. This is not your typical parenting guide, or how-to book. My purpose and goal for this book is to bring awareness to areas from my childhood that I feel needed attention, as it ultimately impacted my transition into adulthood. I realize parents may not think these areas are a big deal, but having experienced them, I know they can possibly have a traumatic influence on any child, if not addressed.

Looking at the condition of our youth today is heartbreaking Being a part of the change is so desperately needed but can sometimes seem as if it's out of reach. Hopefully, by sharing my childhood experiences, I can shed some light on areas that may need more attention and possibly lead to building stronger relationships with parents and their children. This is my way of trying to become the effective change that I would like to see.

As I look at my place in society and the world that I live in today, my heart becomes heavy. I look around and see the conditions of families and their state of mind—African American families specifically. Our youth today lack purpose, direction, self-respect, love, and the list could go on and on. I often ask myself: *how did we get here?* I want so badly to figure out a way to make a difference and to be the change I want to see. Most times, my mind becomes clouded by my own situations and circumstances that stem from past hurt. It is in those moments that I realize some of the struggles and issues that need to be addressed.

Crime rates are at an all-time high; children are without parental guidance. Parents are lacking resources to provide for their children. Fathers are not in the home, and nowadays, mothers are not either. Parents are more of their children's besties than they are their parents. Money, sex, and drugs are a popular lifestyle; babies are having babies, and most alarmingly, God is not acknowledged.

They say history repeats itself, but at what point do we rewrite the narrative? How many children must die? How many families must be separated? How many battles must we lose before we decide enough is enough? I am a product of a lot of these broken situations and have experienced firsthand the hurt, frustration, and setbacks that are attached to these broken situations. I'm sharing parts of my life as a form of release, a means of help, and more importantly, as a guide to hopefully allow parents to see and understand the importance and the necessity of being present in every aspect of their child's life both physically and emotionally. These very children will one day reach adulthood and their success or lack thereof could be contingent upon the foundation that was set for them as children. Ultimately, parents are raising their kids to become successful adults.

With that being said, take a look with me through the lens I see through now as I share my personal perspective on parenting!

Chapter

"We never know the love of a parent 'til we become parents ourselves."

— Henry Ward Beecher

"Super Mom" ... The Perfect Parents

What is a "perfect" parent? Is there really such a thing as a *perfect* parent? My parents were perfect in my eyes, and many of your children feel the same about you. My mother was a super mom! To this day, I am sure they came up with the phrase "something out of nothing" because of the many miracles my mom made happen.

I grew up in the heart of the ghetto. Now, your definition of "ghetto" may differ from mine. When I say ghetto, I am referring to an environment riddled with gang activity, drug and alcohol abuse, fights, shootouts, and dice games. But still, even amid that upbringing, I think about how much fun it was. I think about the neighborhood and how everyone was a family and enjoyed each other's company, from the barbeques, to relay races in the street, to Double Dutch competitions, and dance competitions. I think about how we played at the park all day and when the streetlights came on, we knew it was time to head home or else my mom would stand on the porch and yell down the street, "April, Al—" and before she could even finish her sentence, our friends would say, "It's time for y'all to go home."

I remember block parties and what we called "getting wet" with the water hose on hot days. I remember sitting on the porch and waiting for girls to walk out of our neighbor's house so that we could see the hairstyles. Chell and Shay would slay everyone's hair on the block! My mom would get the special—a cornrow with a side bang and her boyfriend's name written across the cornrow with pearl pins. Whew, that was so ghetto!

I remember attending church faithfully on Tuesdays, Thursdays, and Sundays with our grandmother. We were raised Pentecostal Apostolic so there were certain things we were terrified to do. We pretty much thought if we blinked wrong, we were candidates for hell. The last thing that was on our minds was stealing cars, fighting, drinking, and smoking. Not that it was not happening, but we just never considered it back then. We were real church kids.

I remember walking to the corner store and running up my mother's tab with Mr. Johnson, the store clerk. He would allow my mom a certain tab limit until she could pay it. She would send us to the store to get lunch meat for sandwiches, maybe chips, and something to drink for lunch. We would add Flamin' Hot Cheetos, pickles, Snickers, and Skittles to the written list as we had perfected our mom's handwriting. He would look at the list and then look at us as if he knew mama did not add those extra snacks, but he still gave it to us. When she would get the bill, she would say, "Now I know I did not run this tab up this high."

My mom was kind of overprotective. She really did not allow us to go with many people. However, she had this one friend named Fanny. We called her Pat. My mom would let us go everywhere with Pat. Most of the activities we were exposed to outside of the neighborhood were because of Pat. She kept us involved in events taking place in the city. We also would hang out with my older cousin Gloria. She would take us to the park and bring big bags of chips and juice. We would mix them all together and have the time of our lives. Life was great; at least I thought so. It was not until my adult years that I realized how much my family struggled in various areas.

My mom was a single parent. She became a mother at the age of sixteen. She was the original sixteen and pregnant. By the age of twenty-six, she had four kids—three boys and one girl. Being the only girl was different; you would think that I would be the center of attention, but nope, those boys were spoiled rotten. When I was 13, my baby sister Jasmine completed our family of five. The attention quickly shifted to her, and I felt invisible although we all spoiled her. She was the perfect addition. Let's just say, middle child syndrome is real!

I was always amazed by my mother's strength and resilience. I am sure that's where I get it from. She relied on government assistance for a good portion of her life, but she always seemed to make a way for us. We did not have very many name-brand clothes and shoes but when she could, she was sure to get them for us. We never went without food. My mother made sure the refrigerator and freezer were stacked to capacity. Thank God for food stamps.

I can remember my grandmother's red truck riding past Lafollette Elementary School Park. My youngest brother, Al , and I, would be playing basketball as we did everyday faithfully. As soon as we saw that red truck, we would drop that ball, yell to our friends, *"See y'all later!"* and sprint home so that we could be there to take the groceries in. It was always exciting to look through the bags and see chicken nuggets and chicken patties, chips, cookies, cereal, chicken wings, ground beef, and my favorite cinnamon brown sugar Pop-Tarts. We were blessed to have home-cooked meals. We could always look forward to having breakfast, lunch, and dinner. My mother did her best with what she had. She did not have any college degrees or advanced education, but she made ends meet and provided for her family.

I do not have a lot of memories of my parents together, but I don't ever remember my mom having anything negative to say about my dad—at least not around me. My dad was very smart and gifted. He had an amazing singing voice. Unfortunately, he had his own struggles with substance abuse, but in my mind, he still tried to be the best that he could be to us. I remember in our earlier years going to places like the zoo and Summerfest with my dad and his girlfriend, Quenette. We would also spend nights with him. When we were unable to stay with him, he would still take us to our grandad's house where we loved staying overnight with our favorite cousin, DJ. Their neighborhood was much quieter. My aunt Connie would always order WrestleMania, and my aunt Helen would make the best Kool-Aid and pop 1the best popcorn seeds. It was always good to take a break from all the things that happened on the "block," which is what we referred to our neighborhood as.

My youngest brother and I were not too fond of being away from our mother for long periods of time. We were okay to go if we knew that we would be returning to our mother's house as soon as possible. I can recall one time being with my mom at my aunt Retha's house. My family was known for partying. Everyone loved to party with the Tyler's. There was a big party happening and all the family was there. I do not recall what occurred for my dad to end up coming to the party, but he did. Not only did he come to the party, but he also took me and my brothers from the party, and we ended up over my grandad and aunt's house. My mom was not aware that we were gone; she was just under the impression that we were in the house with our dad. Because we loved being with our favorite cousin, DJ, my aunts, and my grandad, we did not mind leaving with our dad to visit our family as we did frequently.

The problem was, we were not aware that we would be staying overnight.

Now, for my brothers John and Ernest, this was perfectly fine, but this was not okay for me. As the hours passed, and I realized we were not returning to my mother that same night, I had an all-out fit. I cried and cried for hours, wanting everyone in the house to understand the severity of me needing to return to my mother. I kicked and screamed for my mother until my aunt finally called my dad and told him to find my mother immediately. By this time, my mom was aware that we were with our father. She was not happy about it since he did not let her know anything. She came to my grandad's house immediately to pick us up.

My mother and grandmother were our comfort zone. Although we had struggles, we were a very tight-knit family, so we relied on each other for strength and comfort. Now, as an adult and mother, I am beginning to better understand the role of a parent. I realize that sometimes things do not always go as planned. Sometimes life does not go the way you plan it. The road to perfection is continuous. What one individual deems as perfection may be totally different from another individual's perspective. As we learn, there will be some success and there will be some failures. When you have children, you must keep going. You must be the best example for them that you can possibly be.

God has entrusted you with lives that are so precious to him and that alone should be motivation enough for you as a parent to make sure the needs of your children are met. Through all the struggles and hard times, I still believe my parents were the perfect parents. We didn't have a big expensive house and expensive cars. We couldn't afford to wear designer labels and fancy jewelry. We didn't always get what we wanted, and some days, I'm sure it was a struggle for my mom to figure out where the next meal was coming from. However, we never went without.

My mother and father struggled with drug and alcohol addiction. There were times where the addiction was so bad that my mother would give my eldest brother her check so that the bills would get paid. At that time, he was only around 12 or 13 years old. I viewed them as perfect parents because during these trying and challenging times, I had no idea that this was their struggle. It wasn't until my teenage years that I realized the addiction my dad struggled with, and I was an adult when I learned of my mom's struggles. I can only conclude that she was doing her best to keep us protected.

It took learning of my parents' struggles and not previously knowing for me to appreciate how hard they worked at getting themselves together. Most times, it's difficult for me to speak of my mom and dad in the same sentence because while I have memories of being with them separately, I don't have many memories of them being together. Although this could have been a blessing in disguise—as I am sure there were moments I didn't need to see—it was still something I desired.

Sometimes parents do not consider the effects their decisions may ultimately have on their children. There are times that I wished my parents did things differently. I would have loved to be raised in a home with two working parents that were married and had family outings on the weekends. I would have loved a man in the house that my brothers could look up to and learn how to do things like mow the lawn, change a tire, fix things around the house, and provide for a family. It would have been great to learn from watching my father how a man should treat me, what to accept, and what not to accept. There are families whose lives are modeled in this very same way and still are faced with obstacles, but sometimes children should at least be given the opportunity to have that experience. However, you can't change the past, but you can work towards a better future.

Generational curses are real. You can very easily find yourself repeating the same cycle. It is important to address concerns regarding your childhood if you want to see a change in your future. My parents had shortcomings, but they never wavered in their love for us. It is important that kids know you love them, and for the most part, that assurance comes from your actions. Love should be enough to encourage better decisions for the betterment of a child's future. It is important to understand that your children will ultimately be a reflection of you.

Chapter

"Parenthood...it's about guiding the next generation and forgiving the last."

— Peter Krause

Maybe It's Not Their Fault

As I think about some of the encounters that were not beneficial to my upbringing, it leads me to think about the possible encounters that my parents may have faced. What if their thought process or actions weren't necessarily their fault? Do we hold a grudge because they were victims of unfortunate situations? Or do we acknowledge their error, learn from it, and work towards not repeating it? Oftentimes, people repeat the behaviors they have experienced.

For example, I remember having a conversation with my grandmother about her first marriage. My grandmother let me know that her then husband was unfaithful. In fact, he had an entire family on the other side of town. My grandmother was not one for the foolishness, so that ended with his belongings on the curb upon his return. At that time, my mother was only two years old. Although my grandmother remarried and adjusted to a new situation, my mother and uncles now had a new reality of their father not being present.

This situation would later become the reality for my mom and her children. My mom didn't marry; however, I'm sure she learned how to recover from a failed relationship as my grandmother demonstrated that it could be accomplished. As I began to experience relationships, I had an idea of what I wanted as well as what I thought was acceptable and what was not acceptable based on what I witnessed. After a few failed "relationships," I eventually encountered my Boaz (read your Bibles). God had this amazing husband prepared for me to learn from and grow with. As we began to grow, parts of my struggles became exposed.

One of the things I struggled with was my emotions. I really didn't know how to process my feelings and communicate how I felt. My husband would become frustrated early on in our marriage because I didn't know how to verbalize how I felt. I would instead just remain completely silent. I had become so accustomed to this because this is how I was used to coping. What I've come to learn is that this struggle was directly related to the lack of emotion that was displayed to me.

I can't recall many times I was able to sit down and express my frustrations to my father. I know my mom would have been open to hearing me; however, it just wasn't something that was of the norm for us, so I never felt comfortable enough to voice that I needed to talk. I can't say for sure that this is something my mom struggled with, with her parents, however, it didn't seem foreign. As I adopted the mindset of *"Maybe it's not their fault,"* I found myself making sure to note that once I became a parent, I would be sure to free my children of this burden. Looking back, I often found myself angry and frustrated, while growing up, because there were certain moments in my life that I really wished my parents had been a part of it. The reasoning for their absences did not concern me.

The only thing I identified with was the hurt of seeing others supported by their parents while mine were not present.

I was raised very well; my parents and grandmother ensured that my siblings and I were respectful and took care of our responsibility concerning school, so it was no secret that I would be the kid that was involved in everything that called for some form of celebration to acknowledge the given achievement. From elementary school to college, I was a part of honors programs and involved in many extracurricular activities, including sports. There were many times that I received awards with no one there to express how proud they were. Those moments were the most difficult. It is a different feeling when you have someone there in that moment to cheer you on and encourage you.

As I continued through life, I found myself not as motivated at times because I didn't feel supported. What I did not take into consideration was some of the possible reasons that my parents were not physically present. The truth is some of the decisions that life forced them to make contributed to them not being able to show up in the capacity that they may have wanted to. With my father still battling drug abuse and my mom working to provide stability, it did not leave much time for appearances.

My oldest brother, Deondray, once told me the single most important thing you will ever do is make a decision. We know this to be true, because sometimes those decisions are difficult or life-changing, even. In fact, the decisions you make, whether good or bad, will determine various outcomes that you have to deal with. What seems to be enjoyable for a moment could leave a negative impact on your forward progress. For example, I think about the era in which my parents were coming up.

It's no secret that the 70's and 80's were a time where African Americans were largely impacted by the flooding of drugs within our communities. During this era, there were numerous amounts of black families who faced struggles with poverty and lack of resources. For some, crack cocaine was meant to be used to have a good time; for others, it was an escape from life's problems. Either way, I believe the agenda of getting African Americans hooked on the drug was a success. The use of crack cocaine became an addiction in many homes, which led to parents often neglecting their parental responsibilities. Along with the addiction, crack cocaine served as an occupation for many, which landed them in prison. This created a domino effect of children growing up without fathers in the home. Fathers also had a difficult time trying to readjust to a community once released from prison, as the system was designed for them to repeat the behavior rather than rehabilitate.

Although we cannot make excuses for our parents' choices, it is important to consider what they may have had to endure. There were moments where I would become extremely frustrated and depressed because I felt like life was not fair. I look back on aspects of my childhood and remember wondering why my dad was not at my basketball games or why he did not take me to the park or a gym to practice. I often found myself making up stories to share with my peers about how I would hang out with my dad and the many different things that we would do. I find myself tickled at how these stories would be situations that I had wished occurred. It was almost like writing a fiction book.

What I *did* come to realize was how much those situations affected my adulthood. I struggled without a real father figure. Thankfully, I had brothers and cousins who did what was necessary to fill the void. However, there is nothing like a little girl having her father present. As parents, you must find a way to defy the odds when it comes to your children. I can only imagine the trauma that may have been and still is present with my brothers.

We must understand that just because individuals find a way to cope and deal with the situations that are before them, does not mean that it is not a daily struggle. Many time people put on a game face, to cover and hide the trauma they have endured. This is the route the "stronger ones" take. On the flip side, you have those who can't mask or hide what they are experiencing. Some people look for an outlet through unfavorable situations, although it's not necessarily the right thing to do. As a result, we find these situations play out with gang activity, alcohol or substance abuse, sexual abuse, and violence.

Many may not admit it, but youth today severely lack proper parenting. Although we know there are situations that parents may have encountered that may have ultimately hindered their ability to properly connect with their children, like poverty or setbacks in general, it can't be used as an excuse to repeat the cycle. Communication is a vital piece in family dynamics. When a child does not understand why his or her parent is absent (not around or not in tune) the child automatically associates the absence with a lack of love. It's difficult for children of any age to understand how their parents can love them and not be there for them. As parents, it is imperative for conversations to take place so that children can understand some of the intent behind an absence. Perspective is important and what you may think is minor could be major for your child. Hard conversations are difficult to navigate through, but they are necessary. Growing up, my siblings and I were taught to stay in a child's place and that certain adult conversations didn't involve children. Although I agree with this statement, there are some situations where parents need to communicate with their children effectively, as they do with their friends and others. It may not happen on the same level, but both parent and child should be comfortable having a conversation and be able to ask questions.

There were many times I became frustrated with my parents, and I am sure they were not aware of it. I selfishly felt as if everything was their fault. After being bullied at school, coping with emotional depression, and so much more, I was extremely upset with them for not noticing my hurt. It didn't matter to me what they had experienced or been through; what was important was the emotional pain that I was bottling up inside. I was upset because my emotions led me to feel that I wasn't enough for them to overcome their issues and give me the attention that I felt I desperately needed.

This is the mindset of lots of children today. While some parents are struggling with the day-to-day challenges of life, unfortunately, so are their children. It can be difficult to notice the struggles your children encounter when you feel trapped or like you are drowning in your own personal issues. So, how do we address this matter where it can be both beneficial to the parents and children? We must have open communication, and there must be a level of transparency.

Chapter

3

"Children harbor a great many doubts and sorrows that could be eased by a loving hug from a parent."

– Richelle E. Goodrich

Transparency

What is transparency? When you can be transparent, you are able to express your authentic self by revealing that you have nothing to hide. This approach allows you to establish yourself as not only an honest person, but also trustworthy and credible to others. When it comes to relationships, friendships, business partnerships, and most importantly, parenting, it is important that we operate with this mindset. Although we may not always share our thoughts with our children, especially when information can be traumatic, too serious, or too mature for the child's ears, there should be a level of transparency to establish total trust and open communication.

I did not have that openness growing up with my parents. We weren't what I would consider emotional people who expressed themselves through hugs, conversations, and things of that nature. We just kind of knew that in the event we needed one another, we would be there. It wasn't until my adult years that I could remember emotional conversations or gestures. I don't think that this is a terrible thing as different families communicate differently. However, I do feel it is important to know the needs of your children and not just based on your assumptions. There were very few times I can recall being transparent with my parents, and to be honest, that void is why I now strive to build such a solid relationship of transparency with my children. One of the obvious reasons transparency and vulnerability was such a struggle with my parents, I believe, is because I did not feel as if they were ready for the truth about how I felt their personal decisions impacted my life. I wasn't comfortable with the possibility of hurting their feelings or offending them.

For example: I remember being maybe nine or ten years of age, and my dad would come by my mother's house to visit us at random. We never really knew when to expect him, but we were always grateful for the visit. When he came, we would always expect a bag of chips and a bottle of juice or some type of snack. He didn't stay long, but the effort was appreciated.

There was one visit I can recall as if it happened yesterday. We were outside standing on the porch as he approached. My youngest brother Al yelled in excitement, "There goes my dad!" It's funny how we would say "my dad" as if he wasn't all our dad. As he approached, I was not entertained. I remember saying to myself, "He's just going to drop off some snacks and leave." Sure enough, as he made it to the porch, he pulled out two dollars. One was given to my brother and the other to me.

My brother was so happy that we could go to the store while I was disgusted. I intentionally dropped the dollar on the porch to suggest that his gesture was unacceptable. I couldn't find it within me to voice to my dad how disappointed I was that he would bring us a dollar, give us a hug and a kiss, and would make his exit and that would be that until the next time. This would have been a perfect moment to be transparent with my father and let him know that I didn't want or desire the dollar or the snacks.

It was his company that I desired. I wanted to sit and listen to his angelic voice; I wanted to talk about the teams I played against and how many points I scored; I wanted to report back to my friends all the amazing things I did with my dad as they did so often. But because that openness was non-existent, I kept it in. Not to mention the look of brokenness on his face after him realizing my response to his efforts. As such, I accepted the dollar, the hug and kiss, as well as the until next time.

With my mom, it was different. The first time I can remember opening the line of uncomfortable communication with my mom was my senior year of high school. I remember it like it was yesterday. I was finally eighteen and obviously ready to make some terrible decisions. Before I go further let's put this caveat in, I am and was raised Pentecostal

Apostolic, so there were many things that shouldn't take place with me. Fornication was for sure at the top of the list of things not to do. Needless to say, I found myself losing my virginity my senior year of high school. Aside from freaking out from the fact that I was going to hell, I needed to share this information with someone because I just couldn't believe what I had done. The night I made it home from sinning, I immediately called my best friends Chante, Leandrea, and Angie. This was back when three-way calling on the landline was the thing. I had told them what had taken place hoping that they had some advice for me.

Apparently, I was talking louder than I needed to be because my mom overheard the conversation. I wasn't aware that she heard anything until one day we were talking, and she mentioned to me when I lost my virginity and to who. Talk about someone's mouth dropping—I was shocked. I remember asking her how she knew as it would have taken me a while to share that information with her. She let me know that she heard the conversation with my friends.

As I look back, this moment lets me know that I could have been open with my mom, but because it was not of the norm in our family, the thought was uncomfortable for me. That is why I believe the idea of transparency is very important in our relationships. Once that trust and openness is established, I believe more unfortunate mistakes can be avoided.

Recently, I told my mom that I wanted to write a book. I explained to her the basis of the book and how she would be included in it. She was very supportive of the idea. In fact, her response was, "I hope I haven't done anything to make you feel like I wasn't a good parent." At that moment, I decided to go the transparent route.

I told her, "I don't think you were a bad parent at all; you were a phenomenal mother. However, there were a few areas that needed attention and some things I feel could have been done differently." I did not expound further than that; however, I could see that she began to process and think about what those areas may have been. I am sure it not only caught her off guard, but it was the first time she heard me express those kinds of feelings.

That moment was a defining one. It became the steppingstone to expressing myself more, despite the discomfort it may have caused. As I look back, I realize that, without that initial conversation, as crazy as it sounds, I would not have had the confidence to become the woman and mother I am becoming today.

It is always amazing to think how God allowed me the experience of being a bonus mom before blessing me with my own child. If I'm being transparent, I honestly didn't think I would see the day where I would become someone's biological mom, as I struggled with infertility. I've had the amazing opportunity to help parent my now 19-year-old stepson since he was three years old. From three years of age, I've only referred to him as son. You could imagine throughout this time there were many opportunities for practice. My personal childhood experiences led me to take the transparency route with my son as he grew up before my eyes.

From a child to an adult, my son was very comfortable having open conversations with me regarding anything and he could expect that I would be open and honest about my experiences that led to my decision making. The foundation of transparency was set with him at a young age, so we always kept a safe place for conversation and discussion.

Here's the thing: at some point, children become adults. Ultimately, as adults, we cannot rely on the excuses of what transpired in our childhood. Instead, we must learn a better method and act accordingly. We can place the blame on what we lacked, but it will not change the work that we need to put in so that our children can reap the benefits. Why not give our children a head start? If possible, we should eliminate some of the hard work now.

Generational curses will begin to break as you are reading this. There is no better time than the present. Start now.

How can *you* express transparency to your child or parent today?

Chapter

"The greatest gift a parent can give a child is self-confidence."

— Stewart Stafford

Cycles

I can just hear it now; Grammy award-winning gospel musician, Jonathan McReynolds, singing one of his songs entitled "Cycles," and literally, every word resonates with me. He sings about the everyday struggle of literally trying to fight the flesh and fighting old habits and wanting to move forward even when your personal strongholds or cycles threaten to hold you back. The line that gets me every time is when he sings about generational cycles.

We all experience cycles and/or can fall victim to them if we allow them to fester in our lives. To begin to avoid these cycles, we must first recognize what they are and then acknowledge that it is indeed a cycle. The acknowledgment is the start of not repeating them. Keep in mind this isn't an overnight job of unlearning bad behaviors. Many times, it can take months, years, or even a lifetime. Sometimes what we deem as normal, is really a cycle that needs to be broken so that it doesn't have a negative impact on the next generation.

Everything that has been passed down does not necessarily equate to right. There are many instances where we find that our parents and grandparents made the decisions that they made and had the mindset that they did because of what they were taught, or what they experienced. I personally feel that is okay when it's appropriate. However, I am also a firm believer in the concept of when you know better, you do better. There are some cycles that need to be broken and not repeated for children to grow and develop into stable adults. Someone may ask: *Well, what do you mean by cycles?*

A cycle can be any repeated behavior that isn't healthy for our wellbeing, whether physically, mentally, emotionally, or spiritually. For example, allowing things like fear and anxiety to hinder our growth, choosing to remain in toxic friendships or relationships, making impulsive decisions and not slowing down to think them through, resulting in further damage and setbacks. These are all cycles. But they can all be broken if YOU are open and willing to do it.

As a parent, I find myself being conscious of the various experiences that I do not want for my children. Particularly, those childhood generational cycles I've had to recover from. I was a product of a broken home, and although my mom worked hard to prevent us from having to endure the effects of what could have been traumatic experiences, I was determined to make sure my children wouldn't experience a broken home.

With this in mind, I knew as a child that I would be intentional about dating. I would also be intentional about who I wanted to have a family with. Another cycle was being taken advantage of. Most times when you are a good person with a good heart, you don't necessarily see things in a negative light. However, I have learned that if you give people an inch, they will take a mile. There were times that I felt my mom was taken advantage of because she was such a giving person. To break that cycle, I made it a priority to set boundaries to avoid being a crutch for others. Although I find myself still feeling as if I am an enabler, I am at least conscious of it.

These are just some examples of the many things that can occur while parenting and you must be bold enough to say, "This cycle stops here." There are other cycles that are repeated where things occur throughout generations such as molestation, drug and alcohol abuse, domestic violence, and other more severe situations where you find kids growing up and assuming that it's okay because it happened to their parents, grandparents, and great grandparents.

Here's the reality; this dysfunctional display of love, family, and loyalty is costly when children are exposed, especially at such young and innocent ages. It eventually leads to another generation of trauma. It's time for us to stop masking trauma and address it head on so that we can help create a generation that is mentally, physically, and emotionally functional. We must stop throwing sheets over situations and pretending they didn't happen.

The Bible instructs us to train up a child in the way that they should go, not in the way of dysfunctional cycles. As parents, it's okay to make mistakes. The goal is to learn from them and to become better for our children. One of the reasons why these conversations are not being held is because of the stance that was taken by many of our old-school parents and grandparents, and is particularly popular in the black community, and that is the notion that children shouldn't talk to parents on a deeper level or furthermore consider them a friend.

Don't get me wrong. I totally agree that a child should stay in a child's place and respect should always be there. When the lines are blurred, that's when boundaries are crossed. However, some parents don't believe in having friendships with their children and they purposely don't talk to their children as anything beyond mother and daughter or father and son. Think about it. Because "Big Momma" grew up not being able to speak to her parents about things that were bothering her, afraid that she was "overstepping her boundaries," she in turn raised her children the same way. Her children—we'll call them our parents' generations—eventually grew up and withheld information, feelings, and emotions and while some recognized the unhealthiness behind it and corrected that way of parenting, others raised their kids to reflect the same cycles and toxic teachings of Big Momma because it was simply all they knew.

As it finally reached around to our generation and is now trickling down to our children, some families are now a third or fourth generation of repeating cycles and passing down unhealthy coping behaviors through botched parenting. As a result of there being no progress or conscious efforts made along the way, some families suffer from the lack of communication, of being vulnerable with one another, or befriending and enjoying the company of our parents/children, of respectfully sharing feelings and emotions, and where does that leave us? Broken and back at square one. Now there are parents who have friendships with their children and become more of a friend than a parent. This is when lines become blurred. Boundaries must be set for these relationships to work.

See how one cycle from one generation can infect an entire lineage? It's like a grape or apple that has gone bad in the bunch. Though mold starts on ONE apple or ONE grape, eventually it spreads to the others in the bunch and within a few days, an entire vine is damaged. The same can absolutely be said about a family. I cannot stress it enough. We must first recognize our strongholds, toxicity, and hindrances, and then effectively correct and break those unhealthy habits before they break us.

When it comes to this parenting thing, none of us walking this earth has a how-to manual, and generally speaking, there is no perfect way to parent.

However, there is definitely an unhealthy way to parent, and that includes projecting, entertaining, and repeating cycles that, in turn, will cause your child to stumble and fall as they transition into young adults.

Chapter

"A good father is a source of inspiration and self-restraint. A good mother is the root of kindness and humbleness."

– Dr. T.P. Chia

Your Approach

Picture this.

There are three mothers and three young sons in a waiting room. The sons are running around, having a blast, but don't necessarily understand that they shouldn't be doing that. After all, they have never been properly taught the right way to sit in a public waiting area.

Mother A walks over and doesn't say anything. She just snatches her son by the arm tightly and roughly sits him down in a seat, causing immediate tears to well up in his eyes.

Mother B stands up and gets her son's attention. "Baby, we don't run in a waiting area. Grab a toy and come sit with me until the doctor comes out," she tells him. The child does as told.

Mother C is clearly frustrated but doesn't know how to reach her child, so she sits and allows him to do whatever he wants.

These fictional mothers all tried a different approach to contain their rambunctious sons, and while there is no perfect way to remedy the situation, there is an EFFECTIVE way to getting ahold of your child and getting him or her to understand why you are asking them to do something.

Mother A was a bit aggressive, and while she was able to get her child to sit down, she didn't tell him why he shouldn't be running around or why she grabbed his arm. She failed to explain his behavior and correct it right away. Therefore, it's possible that at the next doctor's visit he'll do the same thing.

Mother C showed that her child obviously makes the decisions, and instead of standing firm and teaching her son the right and wrong way, she allowed him to have his way and continue to disrespect and disrupt the waiting room. As a result, who knows what else he'll try to get away with? Unfortunately, even at a young age, he is already aware that his own mother cannot control or correct him. This is especially alarming when you think about our black children acting this way and eventually encountering the real world or the police who aren't so patient, understanding, and forgiving.

Lastly, there is *Mother B* who didn't use force or harsh words to get her point across. She also stood with confidence, explained to her child what he was doing wrong, redirected him, and because of it, he will now break the habit of acting a fool in future settings.

Now, you may be reading and thinking, "Girl, bye! This is not practical! Has she not seen my child's behavior?"

I get it. These methods aren't necessarily the go-to solutions, but they are there to invoke you, the parent, as you try out different disciplinary actions. Correcting a child doesn't always have to end in whooping or cursing or using excessive force. In fact, yelling and lashing out does more harm than good, especially if the child doesn't even know what he or she did wrong.

Another thing to consider is each child differs. As a parent, sometimes you must address each child based on their needs. While one method may be suitable for one, another approach may be needed for the other. Growing up, my mom dealt with each of my siblings differently. I didn't realize it until I became an adult and began to look back on certain situations. While we were all expected to follow the same rules and produce the same results in terms of being respectful and obedient, her approach in dealing with us was different.

For example, my oldest brother Deondray was more independent. He was in a position that forced him to grow up quickly. He had to help take care of his younger siblings and to an extent our mom as well. So, my mother's expectations of him were different. She often relied on him to make sure things were done which he was sure to do. She didn't follow his every move because she trusted his judgment.

With my youngest brother John, she addressed his needs whenever possible. He was the baby, and we all knew it because what John wanted, John was going to get. My mother approached things a little differently with my brother, Ernest. Although she expected all of us to go to school and get good grades, there was a need to be more understanding of Ernest's needs. Ernest was the child who had a strong determination to become the man of the house in the absence of our father. While his heart was in the right place, the methods taken to provide were not beneficial to his well-being.

My mom took a stern approach initially with my brother. He didn't always make the best decisions; however, he really had a pure heart and tried his best to make sure we didn't go without. Some of the struggles that my mom faced, we were not aware of at a young age, however, Earnest and Deondray were. They both had goals to help address the struggles and Earnest's methods weren't always the best, which caused both my mom and grandmother's approach to be what it was. What may have been looked at as favoritism or treating one sibling differently than the other was simply a mother understanding the needs of her children and taking a different approach with each of them to meet their needs.

When dealing with your approach, it is not limited to discipline. How do you approach your child's emotions, their inability to communicate, or even just their struggles of dealing with life? There are so many young children that are engaging in adult behaviors, running away, being introduced to the prison system, and even addicted to drugs and alcohol. I've heard parents say that they just don't know what to do, the children refuse to listen, and the situations are just out of control. I'm saying consider your approach. Sometimes they may need a word of encouragement.

Words are powerful. If you have told your children they aren't going to succeed in life and that there is no hope for them based off generational curses, then this is a great starting point for change! Your words have life. The very thing you speak over your children, is what will manifest. Express interest in your child. Ask about their day and how school is going. Consider being a part of what's going on so they won't attempt to fill that void with things that will lead to negative outcomes.

Commend them on their efforts. If you know they have been struggling with doing the right thing, acknowledge the right things they've done. For the children who are always doing the right thing, don't allow it to be just an expectation, but acknowledge it and encourage them as well. What does your body language suggest when you are communicating with your children? What is comfortable for you may not be the right approach with them. Sometimes we must step outside of our comfort zones for the well-being of our children.

When approaching your child, think about the desired outcome. Think about how this will impact them later in life. More importantly, place yourself in their position. How would you want your parents to address your concerns? Even consider what approach was taken with you. Did it help you or hinder you? Experience is always a great teacher.

Don't give up so quickly. Instead, try a different approach. Misbehavior or misunderstandings can be addressed with a simple conversation and once you and your child are on one accord with expectations and boundaries, most times, it will end positively and effectively. I leave you with this, have you considered how your approach to parenting impacts the success, happiness, and growth of your child? After considering these thoughts, what ways can you improve or better your approach?

Chapter

6

"The best inheritance a parent can give his
children is a few minutes of his time each day."
– O.A. Battista

Listen

One of the most important things you can do for your child is to listen. Yes, you've read that right. We need to listen to our children, no matter what age, and as we listen, we need to fine-tune our ears to be able to listen—not to respond—but to hear and process what is being said. I can hear some of you saying now, "What is she talking about? What if my child is back-talking? I'm not listening to that!"

And I don't blame you, sis, but hear me out. Listening can take place in your everyday routine while you're driving your child to school, cooking dinner, or sitting down watching TV and having family time. Notice the examples given; most times, these examples are not occurring. Try sitting and eating together instead of everyone eating at different times in different rooms. Pick out a day of the week for movie night for everyone. Many conversations are established through these methods. It's okay to put down the phones, step away from social media, and turn off the streaming services, and just listen to your children, whether they're right or wrong. In order to create a healthy relationship with healthy communication, listening must be practiced from both parent and child.

So often, we think that because we are adults, we don't have to listen or give our children an opportunity to explain themselves or talk in certain situations, and that's not cool. Just like we get irritated if someone doesn't listen to us, or allows us to express our feelings as adults, imagine how frustrating it is for a child who is still learning, growing, and trying to understand life. Although I can't recall many times where I had conversations with my parents as a child, I feel like they would have been good listeners.

My mom specifically was very good at hearing us out. We may have still received a whooping if we were in error; however, she gave us the space to explain. Not only that, but if there were a time that we needed to express our feelings as children and as adults, the kind of woman she is, I believe she would not only listen, but also respond in a manner that let us know she heard us as well. I'm sure there were many times with my older siblings that she had to listen to them because some of the situations required her immediate attention. I wonder if we take the initiative to listen before the situations occur, would it then prevent the outcomes we don't want?

"Stay in a child's place!" This phrase can be heard around the world from the mouths of adults. The reality is, no, I don't think children should be listening in on adult conversations and chiming in, but there is also a way to include your child in the know without lines being blurred. Be clear on what listening to them looks like. Have conversations behind your reasoning for listening and wanting to hear them. When we are intentional about the dynamics of our relationships with our children, it yields better results. What exactly does a "child's place" look like? What does that mean? This can vary based on the parent but the idea of ensuring the lines are not blurred and that there is clarity on the expectation of listening is what's important.

Many times, children feel unseen, unheard, and unwanted simply because a parent doesn't listen or try to understand where they're coming from. That can pose major problems down the line, and when it's time for that child to grow up and be an effective adult in the real world, expecting others not to listen or care, it can create a very calloused, closed-off, and selfish person.

When you don't listen to your child, it indirectly teaches them that their opinions, thoughts, and words aren't important. It can also prevent your child from speaking out in normal circumstances, which is an unhealthy way for anyone to express him or herself. As a result, the child may become an insecure and less than confident version of themselves as an adult.

Moreover, you always want to open the floor for discussions with your child to promote a safe, honest, and open environment. What if your child has a secret to tell, or a traumatic experience to share, and you're too busy or simply not interested enough to listen? As a parent, you would never be able to forgive yourself for setting that kind of atmosphere.

Think back to a time when you had something to tell an adult or parent, and they dismissed you. They didn't listen. They may have cut you off, or simply talked over you without the intention to stop and hear you out. Now, think about how you felt in those moments—I'm sure the emotions ranged from dejected, unwanted, lonely, unheard, and unseen. If you don't listen to them, someone else will.

Listening to my children is something I take pride in and will enjoy, no matter the circumstances, no matter how old they get, and no matter the time or place. If my child is comfortable coming to me, then I will continue to build that trust by listening first and *then* providing loving yet practical solutions to whatever they have to say. If listening is something *you* have struggled with before, or something that didn't occur in your own childhood, make the effort to provide your child with a platform to talk and communicate in a judgment-free environment.

With that being said: Alexa, play Beyoncé, "Listen."

Chapter

"It is the sunlight of parental love and encouragement that enables a child to grow in competence and slowly gain mastery over his environment."

— *Felicity Bauer*

Society Says

The Fresh Prince of Bel-Air. Family Matters. The Cosby Show. Good Times. I'm willing to bet you've heard of these sitcoms before, and chances are, you've watched at least a handful of each of them as well. So, what exactly do all these classic TV shows have in common?

They all displayed healthy, loving, and *strong* family relationships. As a bonus, these were Black families, with excellent examples of fathers and father figures. To delve even further, these shows demonstrated a standard for the families of the seventies, eighties, and nineties. When we think about all the parent-children issues that each show encountered and tackled, we can think back to some very serious, funny, and notable scenes. Every mother nurtured in her own special way, and every father was memorable in his own special way. Their approaches varied but the results were the same: the children knew they were loved.

Still, if we went to social media and examined each episode of every show, society would have something to say, whether negative or positive. "If I was the mother, I wouldn't have done this," or "The father is too overbearing," or "Their children were too spoiled for their own good!"

As humans, it's only natural we compare those shows to real-life and real experiences. But regardless of if it's fiction or factual, wouldn't it be nice if every parent had a how-to manual on parenting the PROPER way? No mistakes would be made, no dysfunction would be present, and every child would have the ideal, happy childhood. But let's face it, we're not on a TV show and we can't just say a few powerful quotes in times of trouble and move on. Parenting doesn't work that way.

Like any relationship, parenting takes hard work. It takes practice. It takes time and patience. It takes mess-ups and hiccups. It takes tears, arguments, and apologies. It takes love and forgiveness. Parenting takes all of that and more, and it is up to every mother and father out there to commit to the job, despite what society has to say.

As I reflect on my own life, if I went off what society said, I would have been thrown away. I am a product of the 53206-zip code. A community filled with gun violence, alcohol and drug abuse, and the list goes on. I've watched children be forced to grow up fast because of the home environment and family situations. If children weren't being placed in the foster care system, they were missing school to look after younger siblings. They would eventually become responsible for making sure those siblings had a meal every day, clothes were washed and ironed, and the house was cleaned.

These unfortunate situations caused children to miss out on doing things that children should have experienced. As they become adults, the thought process of living for them is survival mode. This leaves us with another generation of adults who lack the necessary tools and structure needed to properly raise children. My father suffered from drug abuse and my mom was blessed enough to recover. It was stated by family that I would have kids before graduating high school, and a college degree would not be within my reach. Now with this resume, according to what society perceives in these situations, I should not have obtained the things that I have this far.

I decided that I would silence the outside noise and determine the narrative for my life. My parents laid a foundation and although there were mistakes along the way, I was able to recover. The good thing about my story is the good outweighed the bad, but that is not the case for a lot of children. I didn't allow the experiences that I felt impacted my adulthood to frame who I would become. As I am still becoming, I feel responsible for sharing these various experiences in hopes that someone will realize that there is still hope.

Children are often heavily influenced by how they are viewed by society. This is why it is imperative that parents establish meaningful relationships, provide a level of open communication, and ensure that a partnership with boundaries is in place. Unfortunately, if we look at the world we are living in today, one will think that there is no hope for the youth. In the city of Milwaukee particularly, we witness children as young as 10 years old stealing and wrecking cars, taking lives, smoking, and drinking with no consequences. We then must ask ourselves, who do we hold accountable for this behavior? Ultimately, it falls back on the parent. I would personally go so far as to say the community as well.

There was a time when the saying "it takes a village to raise a child" wasn't just cliche. I could remember as a child everyone on our block being responsible for one another's children. My best friend of 30 plus years lived across the street from me. Her mom, Faith, who is no longer with us physically, was so instrumental in my life. Whatever event my mom couldn't make, she was there. Chante and I pretty much did everything together; however, if I was doing something Chante wasn't a part of, her mother would still be there to support me. She literally was a second mom. That was the definition of, "it takes a village."

There were times when my mom cooked and fed other kids in the neighborhood. She wasn't concerned with what transpired for them to be hungry. There was a need, so she made sure it was met. These types of gestures were the norm in my neighborhood. I remember Ms. Carla would make the best nachos and she made sure we had some whenever she made them. If kids were disrespectful, it didn't matter whose parent addressed the behavior, but it was sure to be addressed and no one was offended.

Times have changed drastically. The sense of community is almost nonexistent in many areas. Nowadays, if another adult tries to redirect someone's child, they may end up getting hurt. The reality is: children are being counted out before they even have a chance. Prisons are being built as fast as black children are being born. Society says by third grade, they won't be able to read and write and it will spiral out of control from there. Society says the communities are lacking resources so there's no hope for their future. Society says broken homes are too common and families will continue to rely on government assistance.

So, my question to you is: What will YOU do to break the cycle of societies' perception? In the previous chapter we talked about cycles. As we can see, they will continue to repeat themselves if we don't step up and change the narrative.

Read that again.

Society has a way of making a person feel like their way or their method isn't good enough, and parenting is no exception. You can easily scroll to a video on social media of a parent and child literally doing a cute dance routine in their living room, but the inevitable happens. The internet experts come out of the woodworks, pointing fingers, judging, and chastising. "Does that baby know her ABCs? That child looks too grown-up!" I'm sure you've seen it, and sometimes it may even be true. But as the shepherd and head of your child's life, you must first disregard society's views and understand the kind of child you're raising, and then figure out what method of parenting works best with that child.

Parenting styles are not always the same, in the sense that one way of parenting works with multiple children. You must know the difference and discipline accordingly. For example, I have had many conversations with friends and even coworkers on their approach to certain situations when dealing with their children. While one may feel like using a belt is a little extreme, another feels like if you spare the rod, you spoil the child! One believes in sheltering the children to protect them as much as possible from the different tragedies that occur daily. Another feels as if it's important for their child to experience life to best learn life lessons. Whatever the case may be, your children are depending on you to make the best possible decisions for them until they are able to make those choices themselves.

As stated before, you should always strive to guide and mold your children into the kind of decent adults you would want them to become. Don't let society interrupt your flow or make you feel like what you're doing isn't right or popular. Also, don't let society cause you to lose hope or give up on your children. If anything, be determined to silence the opinions of society. The Bible declares that we can do all things through Christ Jesus who gives us strength. Every household is different, every parent is different, and every child is different. As long as you're providing a safe, loving, supportive, and appropriate home, then you are on the right track.

Chapter

"The Golden Rule of Parenting is do unto your children as you wish your parents had done unto you."

– Louise Hart

Lessons Learned

I strongly believe that the things we experience, whether good or bad, allows us to learn a lesson. Although I was a bonus mother to begin with, I recently became a new mother, and it has allowed me to do some self-reflecting, which includes recalling many of the lessons I've learned. As parents, we go into this lifelong commitment blindly. No matter how many stories we hear; no matter how many children we babysit and return to his or her mother; no matter what we see around us, once we are parents, we are on our own and have to figure it out. There is no slowing down or backing out. This can be extremely intimidating for some who may lack support, which is why I hold strong to the scripture in the Bible that says I can do all things through Christ who strengthens me.

Sometimes we can pull on the expertise of our parents, or friends with children, or even by reading books, but ultimately, we must raise our children how *we* see fit. We must raise our children using the positive reinforcements we didn't necessarily see as children, while trying to avoid generational curses and debunk stereotypes.

I have learned it doesn't matter what your family thinks, your best friend thinks, or what the "expert mom" on the internet thinks. I think it's beneficial to seek advice and as my Bishop would say "use a rake and a shovel," meaning shovel in the good and rake out the bad and when doing so consider: *What kind of adult do I want to raise? What kind of responsible and respectable citizen do I want to raise? What kind of loving future wife or future husband do I want to raise? How can I contribute positively to this little boy or little girl?* These are the burning questions that we must consider as parents.

We must make a conscious effort to do the best we can in expected and sometimes unexpected situations. More specifically, as a mother, I would be doing my children a disservice if I didn't practice what I preached or implemented the same principles that I instill in my adult friendships. For example, would I expect accountability and respect out of a friend? Yes. In turn, I would instill those things in my children. Do I expect honesty and integrity from a friend? Of course.

So, again, I would instill those qualities in my children. My approach would be intentional but loving, knowing I'm helping to set the tone for my children's future. What I teach them now will later determine the kind of adults they'll become someday, and when done effectively, that's a beautiful thing.

What is your child's perception of you? Do you know? Have you ever considered asking your child how your relationship can improve? I was listening to a young man who went live on Facebook to address some concerns he had, as he was being labeled as the cause of another young man's death. In the live video, the young man was very passionate and voiced how he felt that the parents of the youth today are the cause for them dying at a young age. I thought this was interesting as he proceeded to state his reasonings. He further shared that kids are outside at times that they should be home being supervised and parents have no idea where they are. He continued to express that parents are too busy drinking and partying, leaving kids to figure things out for themselves or they are drinking and partying with their kids.

Another thing that was heartbreaking to hear was how he alluded to the idea of parents receiving payments for their children and using the money for their personal pleasures rather than providing for the child. This leads the children to pursue other ways to make money in efforts to buy clothes and shoes to avoid missing school and being bullied. I can only imagine how hard it must be for a parent to hear a child say their actions are the cause of their own young children dying. He even shared how, although he made the choice to not listen to what he was taught, he wished that he had because he now understands why his mom took the approach she did.

Hearing that young man express those things encouraged me to continue writing this book. I not only wanted to revisit areas where I've learned lessons based on the outcome of situations from my own childhood, but to also bring awareness to parents everywhere to pay attention to their children's thoughts and concerns as these are things that will ultimately affect the adulthood of the generations to come.

Many parents may feel as if the damage is already done so they make no effort to correct certain behaviors, but the truth is, allowing it to continue makes matters worse. There is still time. Every experience we go through is not always easy, pretty, or even fair. However, sometimes God's intent is for you to be a light to someone else. I know you're thinking, *"So, you mean to tell me I'm supposed to be okay with the hurt, frustration, and depression*

I've experienced because someone else can benefit from my struggles?" And I'm saying, "Yes!"

That someone may very well be your children. If you know what it feels like to be neglected, that's the last thing you should want your children to feel. If you know what it feels like to be dismissed, that's the last thing you should want your children to feel. If you know what it feels like to be walked out on, that's the last thing you should want your children to feel. As stated in Chapter 6, break the cycle! What if I told you your adult child struggles with feeling inadequate and less than because of the things that were spoken over their life as a child? As an adult, it is difficult for them to get through a job interview because they don't feel capable. They struggle in relationships because they lack communication skills and the ability to love and be loved.

It is important to reflect and ask yourself, what lesson can I learn from this? I've learned so many lessons simply from the test and trials that God allowed me to endure and overcome.

Sometimes you must consider your perspective. What I mean by that is, yes, I've had some unfortunate experiences but instead of being depressed about it, I'm going to rejoice in the fact that God chose me to complete the task because He knew I was strong enough. A perspective check will help you overcome and be a light for the next generation.

Ultimately, you must advocate for your own family. I have decided to take on the lessons I've learned not only from my own childhood experiences, but from observations from my adulthood and apply them to my parenting today. One of the biggest lessons I've learned is that my words have power, and I can be the change that I desire to see. I am honored to be the GPS to my children's lives, with God's guidance, and my husband's unwavering assistance.

Chapter

"It is time for parents to teach young people early on that in diversity there is beauty and there is strength."
— Maya Angelou

Transitions

Life is filled with many changes, including many setbacks and sorrows, as well as many triumphs and victories. Overall, there are many seasons. I don't mean seasons in the traditional sense of summer, fall, winter, and spring. What I mean is the season of transition. As time marches on, we get to see our once little baby boys and baby girls become young men and women. It's priceless. However, because life is not void of hardships or trials, with those kinds of changes comes transitions. Some of these transitions are good and other times they are simply uncomfortable.

At times, I look back and recall the many transitions that took place with my parents—my mother, specifically. I can only imagine the difficulty of going through so many different transitions while trying to parent. Transitions equate to change. Change is not always easy, and many times can lead to states of depression and other factors that will hinder your ability to effectively parent. What's interesting about these transitions is that your children will go through them with you. My mother pretty much got what she wanted as a young girl. My grandmother made sure she received what she asked for. Not to mention she was the only girl, so her brothers took the same approach.

At 16, my mom became a mother, and that was a life changing transition. Eventually she would end up a single mother of five children. On top of being a single mother and trying to provide, she battled drug addiction, which is another transition. So, then there's the struggles of trying to navigate parenting and addiction. Eventually, she was able to escape the bondage of drugs and alcohol and work a job. Soon after, health issues became apparent. This was yet another transition to navigate. I watched as my mother gracefully transitioned from phase to phase and there wasn't a time that I can recall her having a pity party about it. That's why I call her resilient. Unfortunately, these transitions were not just experienced by her, but by my siblings and I as well.

My oldest brother had to deal with the effects that came with my mother having to adjust to a new normal. The process of battling drug abuse caused us to sometimes spend more time with our grandmother, which wasn't a bad thing; however, that meant less time spent with our mom. Recovery and entering the workforce caused us to have to adjust to a working mom whose approach to life now looked different. My point is, when these transitions occur, the children are very much transitioning as well. Having to deal with friends, school, and just life in general, while dealing with so many adjustments can become overwhelming and cause children to shut down.

For my siblings and I, most times we didn't know what was going on because my mom did her best not to expose us to certain struggles; however, everyone is not that fortunate and are exposed to every aspect of the transition. It is important that when life brings about these different transitions that you check in with your children as they are transitioning too. Ask them their opinion, get a sense of how they are feeling, and allow them space to express the impact your decisions have on them. When we disregard the feelings of our children and minimize their role in our lives, it causes them to feel neglected, not important, and without a voice. When they take on this perception, we find that they began to make bad decisions and began to seek out attention from other places.

I'm extremely proud of the woman my mom is today because as I look at the transitions that have taken place in her life, she could have easily given up. There were many times I'm sure she didn't see how she would get through certain situations or may have even regretted certain decisions that were made. She made a conscious decision to make a change so that the next transition would benefit her children. Because she did not throw in the towel, but rather endured the hardship, I was able to benefit from her endurance. Her endurance helped to produce the woman I am today.

I am careful to consider how the transitions I experience may affect my children. My thought process is no longer what's best for me, but what's best for my family. Change is necessary and sometimes much needed. It is important to consider how that change will impact your child's life. If my children are going to have to endure a season of transitioning with me, it will benefit them positively. Sometimes transitions are inevitable, but we can be intentional about how we manage them.

How will your parenting benefit from transitions? Will your parenting grow and mature as your child also grows and matures? Will you fold under pressure when life gets tough? Or will you stick things out and show your children how to overcome adversities?

As parents, we must always wear our game faces. Sometimes life's storms can blow so hard that it's not easy. Sure, it's okay to be transparent and honest with your child if you need to be, but in times of uncertainty and during times of transition, we must also conduct ourselves so that our children can adopt the same optimism and positivity. We must do all we can to prepare our children for life—the ups, the downs, and the in-between days. We must empower, encourage, and educate while showing love, empathy, and direction. Having that balance, along with being a support to your children is the only way they can face transitions and adversities with confidence.

There will be some days where you have no idea what you're doing, and other days, you will feel on top of the world and your child will look at you as if you are their hero. We will always have those days for as long as we live because parenting is truly a rollercoaster, but just don't give up! Transitions will come but it's how you respond that makes all the difference.

Chapter

"There is no such thing as a perfect parent. So, just be a real one."

— *Sue Atkins*

The Outcome

I'm grateful that God provided me with the opportunity to take the challenges and tough times that I experienced as a child and use them as an opportunity to not become bitter, but to become better. It is our responsibility as parents to heal where we may have hurt so that we can be whole for our children. It is easy to place the blame on past traumas and issues. Although our experiences are valid, it becomes our responsibility to change the narrative.

That's what I decided to do. I decided to take all the past experiences, lessons learned, generational curses, cycles, negative thoughts, and trauma, and turn them into steppingstones for my children's success. The line was drawn with me. I made a declaration that the trauma would stop at me and would not be passed on to my children. What I've come to realize is that not only are there many parents who don't realize the effects of not showing up, cursing your children out, and belittling them, but there are also parents that don't want to do the necessary work to repair the damage that is done because they feel it's too late.

I'm writing this book to inform you it's *not* too late. There is still time to repair but we must first acknowledge the problem. There is no age limit or expiration date on reconciliation and forgiveness. I encourage you to do the work. I didn't feel embraced, and I didn't hear the words "I love you" until later on in life; however, it made a difference. My father passed in 2011, and I couldn't express to him the struggles I faced because of some of the decisions he made. That is something that I must work through daily. I found that writing it down helps to release it. His absence was a key factor in making sure my children wasn't exposed to that form of absence and hurt.

I'm sure there are many who have lost parents and don't have the opportunity to express or work through their trauma with them, however, there is still an opportunity for you to acknowledge it and work through it the best you can so that it doesn't show up in your decision-making and parenting. We know there is a need for change, but there also must be a *want* for change.

The outcome for me looks like my children being priority. Children should know and feel like there is always time for them and that they are not a burden but indeed a blessing. As an adult, I found myself needing to address many frailties and insecurities due to areas of lack in my childhood. The thing I love most is that it wasn't too late to address this before passing it on to my children. The outcome for me looks like fostering meaningful relationships, establishing our own traditions, and enjoying the moment. It looks like healthy and whole children that represent a broken curse.

Children that are confident not only in themselves but in the ability to love, be loved, communicate effectively, and realize that success as they see is attainable with present and supportive parents. It looks like setting limits and being consistent with discipline. My children will know what is acceptable and what is not. They will understand that discipline and consequences as well as growth can be associated with bad decision-making. The outcome looks like me being a good role model.

Children will have various individuals they look up to and may model after, but you are the first example they will experience, and you should display what you desire them to model after. The outcome looks like flexibility. It is important to be flexible and be able to adjust based on the need as different situations arise and the style of parenting may change. It looks like loving my children unconditionally. Regardless of behaviors, diagnosis, or attitudes, your love for your children should remain unconditional without limits and contingency.

What does the outcome look like for me? As a 38-year-old first time mom, I stand confident in the ability to properly train and equip my children to become spiritually, emotionally, physically, and mentally prepared adults. Sometimes experience is the best teacher. The goal of this book is to emphasize the importance of being present in every aspect of your child's life. Really showing up and being present physically and emotionally. Those moments that you may think are not as important *are* important!

The lens that I see through now was created from childhood experiences showing up in my adulthood as well as finally becoming a mom after 10 years of struggling with infertility. To know that there are men and women praying to be the parent you have the opportunity to be should encourage you to examine your parenting. My hope is that we can change the generations to come starting with how we parent, prepare them, and equip them.

Unfortunately, no matter how much you try to do the right thing, there will be some that slip through the cracks, and we must give them to God and pray that his will be done. However, if we can contribute to one less unnecessary death, one less unnecessary suicide attempt, one less reckless driver, one less teen pregnancy, one less individual struggling with drug and alcohol abuse, and one less domestic violence case, let's go for it. As stated earlier, it takes a village. With God at the center, we can be helpers one to another, to ensure at least a chance at a promising future for our children.

You've come to the conclusion of this book. You've read it; you've thought things over about your life and your children's lives, and you've learned a thing or two—at least, I hope. Now, it's time to put to work what you have learned.

Remember: nobody walking this earth's surface has the answers and we are all learning each day, no matter how old we are. Make a conscious decision to always support your children, whether they've done wrong or not, and allow room for effective discipline, love, forgiveness, understanding, and accountability. Just as you want the same grace from others, extend that same grace to your children as they learn and grow.

The end goal, now that you have read this book, should be to take those bits and pieces of your childhood—specifically things you thought your parents or guardians could have improved on—and to introduce your children to new ways on how to handle those situations. It is the only way we'll be able to confidently and effectively raise children who will one day become healthy and whole adults.

Keep in mind, there will be days where you "get it right" and other days will call for some regrouping because it looks like nothing is working. And you know what? That's okay. As much as it can be frustrating, there is beauty in the parenting process, as you and your child continue to evolve through all phases of life. Always remember love covers!

You've got this.

"Parenting is a lifetime job and does not stop
when a child grows up."
— *Jake Slope*

About the Author

April Love-Julien is a minister, motivational speaker, and educator. April has found a great passion for finding ways to reach the youth of today.

A native of Milwaukee, WI, she is the wife of an amazing Milwaukee musician, Alexander Julien, and the mother of two amazing sons, Armarion Julien, and Alex Jr. She holds a bachelor's degree in sociology and two master's degrees in education and school counseling. She currently serves as the Dean of Students.

April's firsthand experiences and exposure to unfortunate situations has fueled her drive and passion for effective change with our youth, families, and communities. Her strong and unwavering faith in God has given her the courage to step out as God's mouthpiece and be the change she so desperately desires to see in our world today.